WHEN DINOSAURS LIVED

Apatosaurus

KATE RIGGS

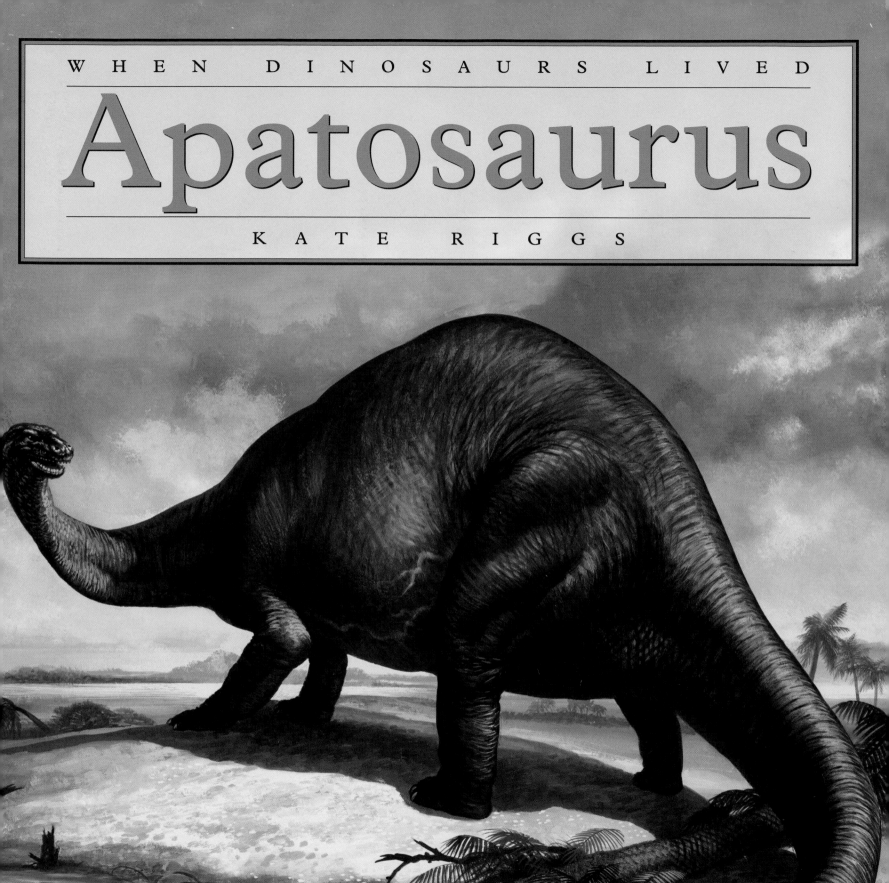

w. francis phillips.

Published by
CREATIVE EDUCATION

P.O. Box 227, Mankato, Minnesota 56002
Creative Education is an imprint of The Creative Company
www.thecreativecompany.us

Design and production by Danny Nanos of Gilbert & Nanos
Art direction by Rita Marshall
Printed by Corporate Graphics in the United States of America

Photographs by Alamy (John Elk III, Eye Risk), Bridgeman Art Library
(English School, Neave Parker, William Francis Phillipps), Corbis (Louie Psihoyos,
Underwood & Underwood), Getty Images (DEA Picture Library), iStockphoto
(Steve Geer, Gilles Glod, Michael Gray, Zoltan Kovacs), Library of Congress

Library of Congress Cataloging-in-Publication Data
Riggs, Kate.
Apatosaurus / by Kate Riggs.
p. cm.
Summary: A brief introduction to the long-necked *Apatosaurus*,
highlighting its size, habitat, food sources, and demise. Also included is a
virtual field trip to a museum with notable *Apatosaurus* fossils.

Includes bibliographical references and index.

ISBN 978-1-60818-116-2

1. Apatosaurus—Juvenile literature. I. Title.

QE862.S3R5523 2012

567.913'8—dc22   2010049633

CPSIA: 030111 PO1451

FIRST EDITION

2 4 6 8 9 7 5 3 1

CREATIVE EDUCATION

Table of Contents

Meet *Apatosaurus*   5

An *Apatosaurus* Life   11

Studying *Apatosaurus*   17

A Virtual Field Trip   23

Glossary   23

Read More   24

Web Sites   24

Index   24

Apatosaurus was a sauropod dinosaur. It lived from 150 to 144 million years ago. The name *Apatosaurus* means "deceptive lizard."

Apatosaurus probably went into water to cool off when it was hot

Apatosaurus: *uh-PAT-oh-SORE-us*

Apatosaurus was a huge dinosaur! It was between 70 and 80 feet (21–24 m) long. It held its long tail up in the air. The tail helped *Apatosaurus* keep its balance as it walked. The tail could also knock down predators.

Some scientists think *Apatosaurus* used its tail like a whip

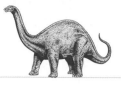

From the time it hatched, *Apatosaurus* grew steadily. An adult *Apatosaurus* weighed about 30 tons (27 t). *Apatosaurus* had a tiny head on top of its big body. The front of its head was filled with pencil-shaped teeth.

An *Apatosaurus* head was about two feet (.6 m) long

Sauropods like *Apatosaurus* lived in or near forests. The forests helped them hide from meat-eaters. *Apatosaurus* found ferns, cycads, shrubs, and evergreen plants called conifers to eat.

Sauropods ate cycad leaves but not the big seeds (pictured)

Apatosaurus used its long neck to reach plants to eat. An adult probably ate up to 1,000 pounds (454 kg) of food each day. Meat-eaters such as *Allosaurus* tried to eat *Apatosaurus*. *Apatosaurus* fought back with its big, heavy tail.

Allosaurus is a name that means "different lizard"

SOUND IT OUT

Allosaurus: al-oh-SORE-us

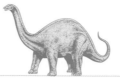

Herds of *Apatosaurus* walked around together. Scientists have found *Apatosaurus* footprints called track-ways that show this. *Apatosaurus* died out about 144 million years ago. Other plant-eaters took its place.

Big dinosaurs left tracks such as these in Oklahoma

Scientists know about *Apatosaurus* because they have studied fossils. Fossils are the remains of living things that died long ago. Many fossils of *Apatosaurus* have been found in the western United States. The first one was found in 1877.

Searching for fossils
can take a long time

Paleontologists are people who study dinosaurs. Othniel C. Marsh was the paleontologist who named *Apatosaurus*. He called it "deceptive lizard"

Apatosaurus compared with a five-foot-tall (152 cm) person

because *Apatosaurus*'s tail bones looked like they could have belonged to a different creature called a mosasaur. Mosasaurs were reptiles that lived in the sea.

People used to think that *Apatosaurus* dragged its tail on the ground and stretched its neck up high into the air. Now people think that its tail and neck were held more even with the rest of its body. But scientists still study *Apatosaurus*. There are more things to learn about this "deceptive lizard"!

Apatosaurus held its head about 17 feet (5.2 m) above the ground

A Virtual Field Trip: Carnegie Museum of Natural History, Pittsburgh, Pennsylvania

You can see an *Apatosaurus* skeleton at the Carnegie Museum of Natural History in Pittsburgh, Pennsylvania. The museum was named after businessman Andrew Carnegie. In 1909, paleontologists from the museum found an *Apatosaurus* skeleton and named it for Carnegie's wife, Louise. The skeleton was displayed as *Apatosaurus louisae* and has been there ever since!

Glossary

cycads—plants that look like palm trees and have big cones, or dry fruit

evergreen—green all the time; evergreen plants have leaves that stay green year round

hatched—came out of an egg

predators—animals that kill and eat other animals

reptiles—animals that have scales and a body that is always as warm or as cold as the air around it

sauropod—a large, plant-eating dinosaur that had four legs, a long neck and tail, and a small head

The *Apatosaurus louisae*
skeleton

Read More

Dixon, Dougal. *Plant-eating Dinosaurs*.
Mankato, Minn.: NewForest Press, 2011.

Johnson, Jinny. *Brachiosaurus and Other Dinosaur Giants*.
North Mankato, Minn.: Smart Apple Media, 2008.

Web Sites

Dinosaur Facts

http://www.thelearningpage.org/dinosaurs/dinosaur_facts.htm
This site has a fact sheet about *Apatosaurus* that can be printed out.

Enchanted Learning: Apatosaurus

http://www.enchantedlearning.com/subjects/dinosaurs/dinos/Apatosaurus.html
This site has *Apatosaurus* facts and a picture to color.

Index

Carnegie Museum of Natural History	23	necks	13, 21
food	11, 13	paleontologists	18, 23
fossils	17	predators	7, 11, 13
heads	9	reptiles	19
Marsh, Othniel C.	18	sauropods	5, 11
name	5, 18	size	7, 9
		tails	7, 13, 19, 21
		United States	17